OUGH DOGS

BULLDOGS

Julie Fiedler

The Rosen Publishing Group's
PowerKids Press™
New York

For Lee, Caryn, and Alex

Published in 2006 by The Rosen Publishing Group, Inc.
29 East 21st Street, New York, NY 10010

First Edition

Editor: Jennifer Way
Book Design: Elana Davidian

Photo Credits: Cover (left) © Greg Stout/Masterfile; Cover (right) © Eunice Pearcy/Animals Animals; p. 4 © Henry Ausloos/Animals Animals; p. 4 (inset) © Gerard Lacz/Animals Animals; pp. 7, 20 © Larry Williams/Corbis; p. 8 Yale Center for British Art, Paul Mellon Fund, USA/The Bridgeman Art Library; p. 11 (left) © Corbis; p. 11 (right) © Getty Images; pp. 12, 16 © LWA-Dann Tardiff/Corbis; p. 15 © Tim Davis/Corbis; p. 15 (inset) © GK Hart/Vikki Hart/Getty Images; p. 19 © Sean Murphy/Getty Images.

Library of Congress Cataloging-in-Publication Data

Fiedler, Julie.
    Bulldogs / Julie Fiedler.— 1st ed.
      p. cm. — (Tough dogs)
    Includes bibliographical references and index. ISBN 1-4042-3119-6 (lib. bdg.)
    1. Bulldog—Juvenile literature. I. Title.
    SF429.B85F53 2006
    636.72—dc22
                                        2004028775

Manufactured in the United States of America

Contents

When talking about bulldogs, people usually mean English bulldogs such as these (above) or American bulldogs. Right: The French bulldog is a different breed of dog.

Meet the Bulldog

Bulldogs are a loving **breed** of dog. Some people believe that bulldogs are **dangerous**, but that is mostly because they do not know the breed well. There are several different types of bulldogs, such as American bulldogs, English bulldogs, and French bulldogs. This book will look at the English and American bulldogs.

Today bulldogs make wonderful household pets and enjoy playing with their owners. Their friendly nature makes them good with children as well as with older people. Some owners also train their bulldogs for cart pulling, which makes use of their strength. They also track, or follow, scents of people or other animals. Bulldogs can sometimes be stubborn, but they are usually **obedient** and can easily be trained. A properly trained bulldog can be a joy to have as a pet and helper. This book will show you the wonderful world of the bulldog.

The easiest way to recognize bulldogs is by their flat, wrinkly faces and their short, thick bodies. Folds surround their short snouts. Adult bulldogs usually have more wrinkles around their snouts than do the puppies.

Bulldogs are very strong and sturdy. They are usually only 20–28 inches (51–71 cm) tall, but they can weigh 60–120 pounds (27–54 kg). They have thick heads, saggy jowls, round bottoms, and barrel-shaped chests, which means that they are large and round. Their short, stocky legs stand wide apart, and their eyes are set deep in their heads. These medium-sized dogs are very strong. Some have pulled more than 50 times their own weight!

Puppy and adult bulldogs have short coats that can be different colors, such as white or brown. They do not have special markings but can have spots or can be a solid color.

A bulldog puppy (left) has markings like an adult bulldog's (right). Bulldogs get heavier wrinkles and skin folds on their faces and necks as they grow into adulthood. Bulldogs have short, strong bodies. They are not as active as other breeds, which means owners must take extra care in watching their bulldog's weight.

The banddogge is talked about in William Shakespeare's play Henry IV. It is on the far right in this painting of a scene from the play. Banddogges, ancestors of the bulldog, were used to fight bulls and bears for sport.

8

Ancestors of the Bulldog

More than 15,000 years ago, dogs were different from the ones living today. They were larger and were not **domesticated**. People began domesticating these early dogs, and they became the **ancestors** of today's breeds. The bulldog's ancestors were used as fighting dogs as well as hunting dogs.

Alaunts were one of these ancestors. They lived in Asia during the eighth century B.C. These dogs fought in battles and were brought to other parts of the world, including Britain, around A.D. 400.

In the 1500s and 1600s, **fierce** ancestors of the bulldog known as banddogges lived in England. The British playwright William Shakespeare wrote about banddogges in his play *Henry IV*. These ancient dogs were **bred** for their strength, bravery, and fighting ability. They are believed to be the ancestors of some of today's breeds, including the bulldog and the mastiff.

History of the Bulldog

Bulldogs as we know them today started to appear in the 1800s in Britain and the United States. At this time people bred bulldogs for dog fighting. Laws banning dog fighting began to be passed in Britain in the 1830s and in the United States in the 1860s. Bulldogs almost became **extinct** around this time because they were considered too dangerous to be household pets.

Luckily, a few people decided to try to breed bulldogs to be pets. By breeding the gentlest bulldogs together, over time this breed became more gentle natured. This led to bulldogs becoming more popular.

Bulldogs began to compete in dog shows in the late 1800s. In 1890, the Bulldog Club of America was formed to make this breed better known. As a result groups such as the American Kennel Club created standards of appearance and **temperament** by which bulldogs are judged. The bulldog remains a popular pet.

Bulldogs have long been popular show dogs. The poster on the left is from the 1902 Chicago Kennel Club Dog Show. It shows a woman petting a bulldog. Above: Beauty was a prize-winning dog of the London Bulldog Society.

Bulldogs are usually very friendly and like to be around children. This is one of the reasons they are popular household pets.

Bulldogs Today

Bulldogs are one of the most popular breeds in Great Britain and the United States. In 2004, there were more than 19,000 bulldogs listed with the American Kennel Club. Bulldogs like to be around people and are especially good with children. Bulldogs continue to compete in dog shows and obedience contests. Many famous people have owned bulldogs, including actor Adam Sandler, actor Ice T, playwright Tennessee Williams, and President Woodrow Wilson.

Bulldogs are also one of the best breeds for **pet therapy** because of their gentle and friendly natures. They enjoy attention and will calmly visit people in hospitals and nursing homes to cheer them up. Sadly because of the dogs' tough appearance, some people are scared by them and believe they are mean dogs.

A Tough Breed?

Some people believe bulldogs are dangerous and are afraid of them. Bulldogs are powerful, but they can also be gentle and loving. Some irresponsible owners train bulldogs to be attack dogs or for fighting. The use of dogs for fighting is illegal. Other owners mistreat bulldogs, which can make them behave **aggressively** out of fear. Because of their strength, bulldogs make good guard dogs. Owners must be careful when training them for this purpose so that bulldogs will only act aggressively if there is a real danger. Properly training a bulldog is important so that owners help ensure the safety of their bulldogs as well as other dogs and people.

DOG SAFETY TIPS

- Never approach a dog you do not know.
- When meeting a dog, offer the back of your hand for the dog to sniff.
- Speak softly, not loudly. Move gently, not suddenly.
- Never try to pet a dog through a fence.
- Never bother a dog while it is sleeping, eating, or sick.
- Do not pull at a dog's fur, ears, or tail. Never tease or hit a dog.
- Never approach a dog that is growling or showing its teeth. Back away slowly. Yelling and running can cause the dog to chase you or act aggressively.

A bulldog who is cared for and trained properly from puppyhood can be a loving pet. Right: Some irresponsible owners treat their dogs badly by doing such things as keeping them in small spaces or training them to fight. This can lead dogs to act aggressively.

15

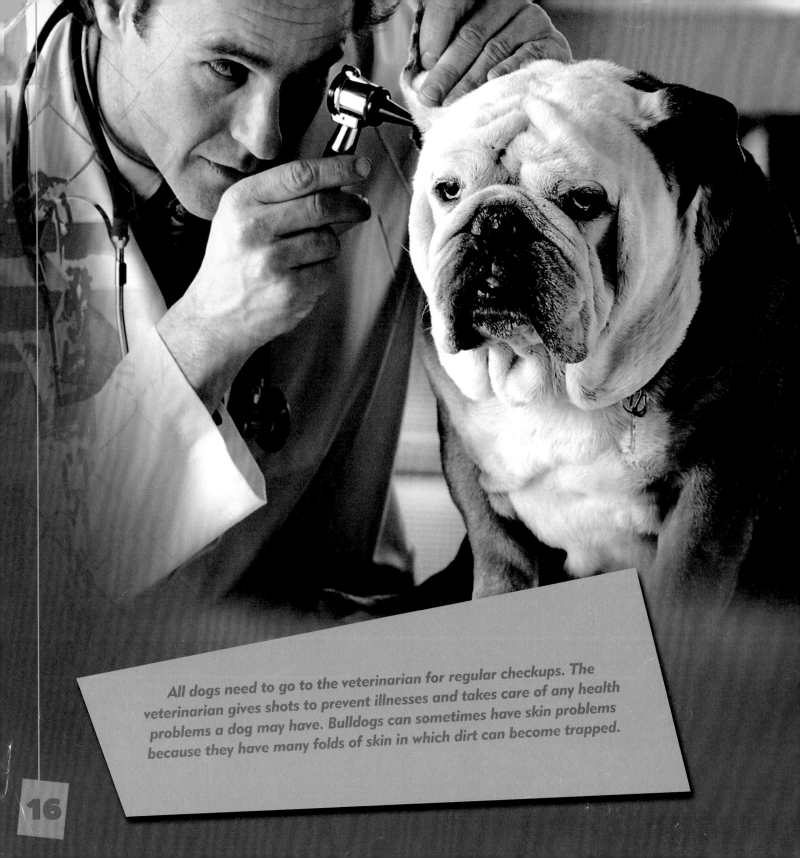

All dogs need to go to the veterinarian for regular checkups. The veterinarian gives shots to prevent illnesses and takes care of any health problems a dog may have. Bulldogs can sometimes have skin problems because they have many folds of skin in which dirt can become trapped.

Giving good care to any breed of dog requires providing shelter, healthy food, water, exercise, love, and obedience training to stop bad behavior. Owners must brush their bulldogs every day and check their wrinkles for dirt or skin problems. Most bulldogs enjoy taking baths, so it is not hard to keep their coats clean. Owners must also make sure their dogs visit the **veterinarian** for regular checkups.

Bulldogs can have some health problems. They can sometimes have poor eyesight. Because of their flat snouts, bulldogs also drool and tend to snore. Their bodies can overheat and chill easily, so owners should be careful taking their bulldogs into hot or cold weather.

Although bulldogs are not very active, they like being outside and need exercise to stay healthy and not become overweight. They should be taken for several short walks during the day.

An important part of raising healthy bulldogs is **socialization**. Socialization means bringing dogs into contact with different people, places, and dogs with careful guidance. It is important to bring young bulldogs into contact with many different sights, sounds, and smells. Adult bulldogs are more likely to be good around new people and dogs if they are properly socialized when they are puppies. Bulldogs like having a **routine** and owners should make socialization part of that routine.

Dog care specialists say bulldogs should start obedience training when they are about six months old. Owners should know how to train their bulldogs properly and must be firm and in control at all times. Otherwise their bulldogs might not listen to them. When bulldogs do not respect their owners, they can misbehave. If owners want help with training, they can take their dogs to obedience school.

When properly socialized a bulldog (far right) can enjoy meeting and playing with other dogs and people. It is important, though, that owners watch their pets closely when bringing them around new animals and people.

Bulldogs work well in pet therapy because they enjoy spending time with people and are often calm, friendly dogs. In pet therapy dogs visit people in hospitals or nursing homes. These visits, in which a dog often just sits with a patient, can make patients feel happier.

Famous Bulldogs

There have been many famous bulldogs in history. Soldiers during the **Civil War** raised a bulldog named Sallie. She stayed by their sides whether the soldiers were in battle or doing drills at camp and helped keep their spirits up.

Another bulldog, named Goldie, liked her neighbor, who was an older man. One day Goldie ran to his front door and started barking. She did not stop until her owner came to see what was the matter. The owner found the old man lying on the floor trying to reach the telephone to call for help. Goldie helped save his life.

A bulldog named Tyson became known for his skateboarding skills in Huntington Beach, California, in 2004. Tyson also walks and skates in benefit events. He is a friendly dog and even plays "big brother" to a litter of kittens at his owner's home. Tyson is a great example of the fun and loving nature of this breed.

Bulldogs certainly have it all. They are friendly, strong, and brave. Bulldogs help people through pet therapy and are well-loved family pets.

Kelley Boy was a beautiful bulldog who became a winning show dog in the 1990s. He was also a therapy dog who enjoyed visiting with patients at nursing homes. One patient he visited would not speak to anyone. Kelley Boy's gentle nature helped bring her out of her shell. Kelley Boy brightened her day. When she saw him, she petted him and said, "Good dog!" Those words were the first she had spoken in a long time. Because of Kelley Boy, the patient was able to start connecting with others again. Kelley Boy is a great example of this fine breed. Now that you know more about them, you can help teach others about bulldogs.

Glossary

aggressively (uh-GREH-siv-ly) Acting ready to fight.

ancestors (AN-ses-terz) Relatives who lived long ago.

bred (BRED) To have brought a male and a female animal together so they will have babies.

breed (BREED) A group of animals that look alike and have the same relatives.

Civil War (SIH-vul WOR) The war fought between the Northern and the Southern states of America from 1861 to 1865.

dangerous (DAYN-jeh-rus) Able to cause harm.

domesticated (duh-MES-tuh-kayt-id) Raised to live with humans.

extinct (ek-STINKT) No longer existing.

fierce (FEERS) Strong and ready to fight.

obedient (oh-BEE-dee-ent) Willing to do what you are told to do.

pet therapy (PEHT THEHR-uh-pee) When people use animals to help them deal with certain problems.

routine (roo-TEEN) When someone does something the same way over and over.

socialization (soh-shuh-luh-ZAY-shun) Learning to be friendly.

temperament (TEM-pur-ment) Character, nature.

veterinarian (veh-tuh-ruh-NER-ee-un) A doctor who treats animals.

Index

Web Sites

Due to the changing nature of Internet links, PowerKids Press has developed an online list of Web sites related to the subject of this book. This site is updated regularly. Please use this link to access the list:
www.powerkidslinks.com/tdog/bulldogs/